ISBN 978-1-946433-71-8
First Edition, First Printing, 2021
Edition of 800

Ugly Duckling Presse
The Old American Can Factory
232 Third Street, #E-303
Brooklyn, NY 11215
uglyducklingpresse.org

Distributed by SPD/Small Press Distribution and by Inpress Books (UK).

Cover design and typesetting by Rebekah Smith and Wen Zhuang,
with Stephen Rosenshein
The type is Arno Pro and ITC Franklin Gothic
Books printed offset and bound at McNaughton & Gunn
Covers printed offset at Prestige Printing and letterpress at Ugly Duckling Presse

The publication of this book was made possible, in part, by a grant from the National Endow-
ment for the Arts and by the continued support of the New York State Council on the Arts.
This project is supported by the Robert Rauschenberg Foundation.

Upper Volta

Ugly Duckling Presse
Brooklyn, NY
2021

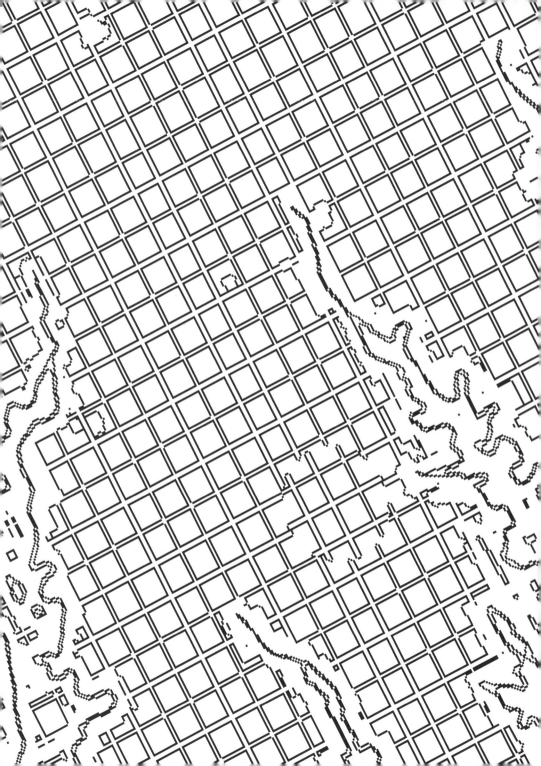

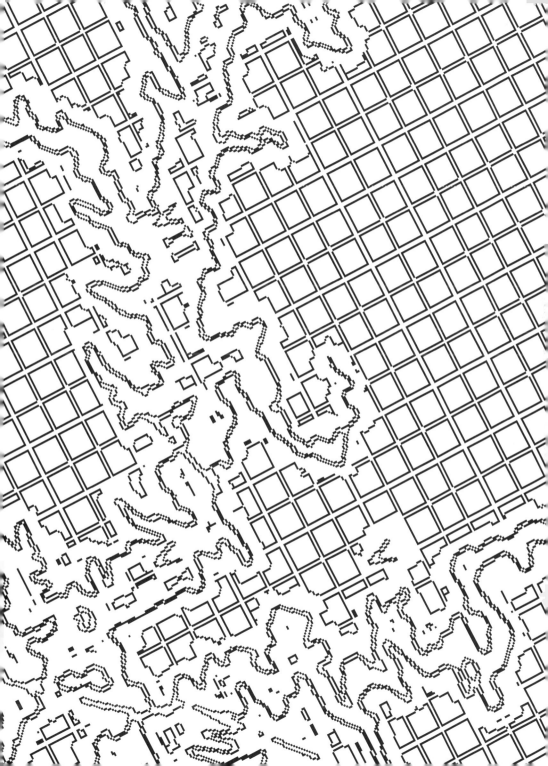

Upper Volta

Yanko González

translated by Stephen Rosenshein

He is born and Busquets, Seckel, Lumsden furnish his bronze crib; the Prat house, the French house or the Scottish house sends the clothes he wears; Krauss sends a car full of toys, chauffeured by the English nurse. He grows and the French fathers or the English Institute takes charge of his education. Tesche, Ivens or Conrado sells him his schoolbooks. Pujol, Pinaud, Cerri, Delteil, Geue, Biagini, Serveau, Dufresne, Cornaglia, Falabella, Russo, Ouvrard or Casini makes his clothes; Pepay, Vuletich, Canguilhem, Rouxel, Werneburg, Ancich, his shoes; Launay, Cohé, capellaro, Voigt, La Joven Italia Wieger, Chopis, Wegener, Haudeville or Biaut, his hat. Diener, Hume or Melrose sells him his soccer or tennis balls; Pabst, Silberstein, Wageman or Kähny his cigars; Weir, Scott, Stirling, or Hayes his liquor. He deposits his money in the Deutsche Bank, the Italian bank or the Spanish bank. Opens his safety deposit box with Söhrens or Bash; insures his life with Equitable Life Assurance Co. or New York Life Assurance Co. His home with Royal FIRE Assurance co. or Lancashire Sure Co. He buys his furniture from Elliot Rourk, Bruhn, Giordano or Muñecas. Muzardhue and Fallay or the Riojana sells him his rugs, Bercciani his curtains; Styles and Slutzki his stove; Gleisner, Barabino, Dabadie, Limozin his pots and pans; Séller or Daneri his lamps; Morrison or Cucurull his toilet; Biancheri or Mondito his china; Vacarezza, Castagneto, Capurro, Porcile, Rovano or Ramsay his groceries; Kirsinger, Doggenweiler or Golz his piano; Ledermann, Bardeua or Douzet his car; Coudeuu camalez, Liebe or Placier the reins for his horses; Coppeta or Tisné his automobile; Moutier, Fritz or Lebeuf, his medicines; Waak, Emmanuel, Weil und Becker, Müller, Hüber, Levy, Meylan, Gauret, Jacob, Umaluf, Köhler, Godart, Ghiringhell, Houluigue his watch and winders; Grote or Mattas his ties; Guillerat, Botín or Wanauld his shirts; Mautier or Mèriot his gloves; Curlet or Chirwing his typewriter; Chanalet, Boschaner, Depret or Texier his lawyer's iron. He buys his paintings from Schlak, Dell'Orto or Strozzi; his spectacles from Strautvetter or Eiter; the volumes for his library from Nascimento or Baldrich; binds his books at Dietsch or Schram; buys his photography equipment at Hans Frey or Durandin; cuts his hair and shaves with Jardel, Cantelli and Cascini or Brun; has self-portraits done by Spencer or Heffer; Weber, Siemens und Schukert, Yahn or Raabellet installs his electric lights; he rides the Chilean Electric Tramway and Light Co. Ltd. trolley cars; he goes on holiday and takes St. Louis Car Co. trams; lodges in the Royal Hotel or the English Hotel in Valparaíso; sails our coasts with the Pacific Steam Navigation Co. Finally, if he dies, Boher or Forlivesi sends a coffin, transports and stuffs him, and Ceppi or Botinelli transcribes on his marble gravestone the Latin phrase Requiescat in pace. (Tancredo Pinochet Le-Brun).

example

They want me to leave as if I did not want to
So I tell them I'm going
But by the first
or fifth step
They come running to find me
to iron their air
Dig them a ditch
where they must cross dresses.

In the village churchyard
there grows an old yew,
Every spring
it blossoms anew:

Old passports
can't do that, my dear,
old passports
can't do that.

(W.H. Auden)

Yesterday was the same
I understood clearly
they want me to leave
this is what they discussed as I cared for their
children

I played what was played in Upper Volta
Example
The chair is called sink the door sardine
The table plate and the shoes *cadira*
So the children shouted
Yellow
Open up the sardine.

It was a game and they told me go
That I had to teach them the words
As they should have been

Example
opening the mouth
is called
laughing.

I

veins for his blood
tumors at noon.

has tea lacks piety.
his father grows.

asks hello you
if there's extra if

there's hunger
a leftover or two .

his mother's nails
saliva at noon

he'll step foot in Peru.

In every land, the universal vices and ills of mankind and human society are attributed to the particular locale. I have never been in a place where I have not heard: here women are vain and fickle, they read little and are poorly taught; here people are nosy about others' business, are chatterboxes, and rumor-mongers; here money, favor, and vileness can accomplish anything; here envy rules supreme and friendships are shallow—and so it goes; as if elsewhere things were different. Men are miserable by necessity, and are resolved to believe themselves miserable by accident. (Leopardi).

that does not want

"that
does
not
want
to
die
like
a
dog
no
one
wants
to
die
like
a
dog
all
man
kind
deserves
not
to
die
like
a
dog
has
lived
like
a
pig
and
does
not
want
to
die
like
a
dog."

"I came to see my friends," they heard me yell through the telephone, furiously covering my other ear.

(e. dobry).

No,
of course you can stay
but it happens
that's to say the house is
let's say that there is not
a lot where one
or two can let's see
it's that I'm in a rhythm
I mean at the same time
with this over there
with the other I would rather
No,
of course you can stay
but it happens
that's to say the house is
let's say that there is not
a lot where one
or two can let's see
it's that I'm in a rhythm
I mean at the same time
with this over there
with the other I would rather
No,
of course you can stay
but it happens
that's to say the house is
let's say that there is not
a lot where one
or two can let's see
it's that I'm in a rhythm
I mean at the same time
with this over there
with the other I would rather
No,

L

that which connects

that which connects propels and turns him
his eye snaps to the target while those below
run towards a new game.
he has seen them all: he plans:
the one that leaves you face up
the one that vomits on your canker
the one that screams into your membrane
the hell of the peasants the cavity of the ancients.

I see my mother grab for the handles and come up short
I see my father smoking fast reading the warnings
my brother assesses me a blow to the stomach strongly
while I stain him with my cotton candy.

the happiness ha ha ha ha the duo sings
posing on a flying swing
that your love gave me // today I want to sing
I pass a long time thinking why we never laugh
better not get into that.
last feast of the festive.

now we want a bicycle
my brother a road bike and I a *BMX*
we sweat phlegm to reach the park
far much farther than Upper Volta
my father said it wasn't easy
and turns up carrying a giant bear.

In other words
he was shoveling feces for many years
although   come on
we all called him the shit-shoveler
that translated to his language might be
cold shower or stone-shoveler.

Let's agree that the shit is memory
in the same way that a word
is the memory of its significance
he kept on making himself the focus
opening or closing the weight of oranges
by anne michaels with drawings by john berger.

But come on
a Shitty Job
on top of that on the black market like the black shit
how to explain it in our language
it could translate as
a "genuinely" thankless job.

And although he used a suit gloves mask and a lovely
green helmet
he stank
on the inside and outside
in fact I was the one that named him
inside&out that in our language
means something like
the fetid external overshadows the fetid internal
amalgamating into the extreme stench.

The point is that he spent his good years
absorbing that
and as it's already known
although the flies change
the rocks will always be the same.

And from those sentences he released
as if for his future redemption
an obvious fatal exhaustion persisted
automatic words rod gauge coupling
monkey wrench residency document maybe fifteen.
A lot of shit.

He published something
and returned to Upper Volta
but he smelled bad
his family dubbed him the "white shit"
that more or less comes to mean without certainty
retreating from or approaching the semantic field
the one who worked as a poet
for those who bring
or take away the wheat
from our mouth.

In other words.

heribert barrera

there are many ways to make men unhappy. one of them is visiting.

gaston miron

one day I will agree to my birth

When we hoisted the flag it occurred to us that fate can also get us there
Not to say that this was ending poorly that your friends have lost heart
that it's not true that one and only truth: *un jour j'aurai dit oui á ma naissance*

You know when we hoisted it we saw the other side (that's *Québécois* enough to get
  us there)
Behind the same rivers the same blanketed black and blue with eyes underneath reality
The ambulated eyelids and a harsh splintering alphabet for the tongue to enter

Father refused to hoist and ripped off a piece of his leg so as not to leave to enter
He said the south which has to be softened which has to fall which had to die
But he was outside and his voltage passed quickly between the air's atoms. Poor thing.

As we cover what is dying we dump it at the foot of the pole we couldn't fix the iris
  the eyelash
It wasn't anyone in particular the mist swallowed it wasn't anyone a sad father
Sad. Sad like a dead father sad at the foot of a pole hoisting a sad flag.

Q

marseillaise

first verse assimilate to place her sponsor to control her
console to alter her second verse offer him to seek him under-
stand him to work him confuse him to translate him third
verse register yourself to indulge yourself memorize yourself
to come yourself seek refuge in yourself to transmit yourself
fourth verse purchase it to insert it award it to permit it fifth
verse to exploit it to expatriate it to plunder it sixth verse.

R

forgermansitisevengoodtohavesomewhatlengthywordsin
theirmouth, fortheythinksslowly, andtheygivethem
timetoreflect.

What little honesty there is among writers. It is evident
in the outrageous way in which they misquote from the
writings of others. I find passages of my work completely
disfigured (...).

The French, even the Academies, give insulting treatment
to the Greek tongue. They take words from her to disfigure
them: they write, for example, *etiologie, esthétique* (...), also
Oedipe, Andromaque, etc.; that is to say, they write the Greek
words as a French farmhand would who had heard the words
pronounced by others (...) To see the Greek tongue mistreat-
ed in favor of a slang as repugnant as is their French (this Italian
spoiled in the most loathsome manner, the long and repulsive
final syllables and the nasal sound) is a spectacle compara-
ble to that offered by a spider from the West Indies when
it eats a hummingbird, or a frog when it engulfs a butterfly.

What little honesty there is among writers. It is evident
in the outrageous way in which they misquote from the
writings of others. I find passages of my work completely
disfigured (...).

beauty is Greek. but the consciousness of it being Greek is Chilean.
nothing is, everything others.

leave

for juan pablo gómez

he leaves a record with the police. resolves leaving a record with the police. change what it may he says I am the type that puts a record with the police if something happens if they harm me. if they mock me for my language. no, no. I leave a record with the police. it costs nothing you stay calm he says a step more a step less. illustrates with his niece in pittsburgh his neighbor in lleida. not with lawyers not with shysters leaving a record with the police. that if things go off. that if the shit hits the fan. to the one stuck at the border, he recommends leaving a record with the police. in his experience there is never a line. not in matucana nor in any other country. that they wait in custody that they implore, I am from outside and I come to instill a record with the police. and they'll find you a room that it's worth it. he thinks it's about measuring them up. after only after looking for work. selling smoke. but he goes back. but he repeats doing no such thing. of not getting across. of not letting it be. of not heeding what he said about the police.

exhaust

When it crawls along we get to say "It's On Its Last Leg"
That it is empty headed that it can't say no to the bread that fills it
And keep hacking opening it stuffing it
Dismembering its motor skills

Turkey on Christmas.

mercat de las flores

for martín g. & pablo méndez

in the front seat: the gambarottas. in the back: the gonzálezes. being neither of the two
he was laid out in the back.

Making himself the gonzález at last.

Ladies and gentlemen, I have boarded

as he arrives at the dive bar, seeing his curly arab hair bags under his eyes

this bus to make a living because I do not

they mock him they mention his mother's pussy.

have a job and I do not have a job because

he hides, continues on his way whistling.

I don't meet the following requirements:

but inside he is dying

I am not Peruvian; I have caucasian fea-

OR WHAT WERE YOU THINKING.

tures and not dark skin I measure six foot

three and not four foot eleven (…) (Aedo).

W

To photograph us and see us in movement on his little giant screen
A good idea for whoever prefers his body double to his own hideous figure
Whoever sniffs and is overwhelmed by the acidity of his three pairs of armpits
Idea good idea for those who whiten themselves.

Something like a *Voyeur* of the gums
A Snooping ocular balloon

Second hand buoy for ghosts.

> The Chilean workers live in huts near the landowner's house, or in the fields where they watch the livestock (…) The Chilean farmer does not come in contact with the German, the wave of democracy has yet to touch these regions (…). (…) These people are dirty, ragged, coarse; their wood huts line the sides of foul paths (…) the huts are divided in two: kitchen and bedroom. In the middle of the kitchen, there is a constant fire that fills the hut with smoke. Around the fire there are always benches or tree trunks on which the Chileans pass the majority of their existence smoking and gossiping. In no part of the world do they lie and curse so often as around a Chilean stove. Their clothes and bedsheets are full of fleas. Outside, the chickens, the dogs and the pigs roam freely among the piles of empty shells and other trash (…). Originally, the Chileans had as much land as the Germans and above that the advantage of knowing the country very well. But while the Germans progress often with the Chilean workers, the man of the earth who works only for himself falls on hard times. He is disorganized, ignores saving, sells his land to drink the profits and falls rapidly into a crippled condition. The majority of these people are liars and thieves and nothing is safe with them. (Leonhardt).

from cashier at HIPER they promoted me to boss
of vegetables for my way of returning the exact change
this skill to cut through red tape and spruce up
the bruised melon / the spoiled vinegar.

tranquil skill of silently finding
in the mesh of a kilo of soft potatoes
that shameful yagana
like this with the long fingernail / I broke the string split
the tie
and threw out the carrot avocado the dawdling lettuce

what fine surgery / what odontology /
b u t w h a t t u n i n g
but to have seen me / WHAT PENMANSHIP.

the little Chileans didn't get it the stockers fucked with me
in Neuquén nothing grows they stir the cider
with cooking gas.
but *cho* / but *yo* / I carried on /
the war of the desert
the vegetable boss from the lost pampa
filling my basket with rotten fruit.

what grace / what an aisle / what a gorgeous ranch
this Argentine slut's
who took the job
from the Chilote in the deli

what a tart / what a heroine
that accused the Mapuche
of stealing from
the bakery.

Y

The one out for a walk takes solace in the image the window projects
He doesn't know it's not him that the glass reflects
That the transparency doesn't steady his liquid figure

all the foreign tongues

But he keeps on posing for an endless photo
Composing of himself a thing that birth never produced
Balancing his flesh on one foot then the other
With his cornea denying his cracks

inspire in me a sacred rancor.

As if the light not matching wasn't enough
He moves his head to the frequency that suits him best
But the message that the radio deafly broadcasts
Is the effigy: same image same voice
That the big boss himself evades.

(E. Lihn)

proverb

but put yourself in my place but
it's that put yourself in my place is
what I'm telling you put yourself in my
place do you find it fair that
he doesn't put himself in my place and
he asks only that I
make the effort of putting myself
in his place without bothering
to even put himself in my
place and ask and ask and ask
that only they put themselves in his place
god bless, what a mess *he who*
was white although he was catalan.

it's that

for coke z. & carolina o.

Chile ... ? he yells at you / doesn't talk to you / no
we hadn't mentioned anything

to

it's that it's true / it's not the accent

we'd have already told him

what makes me uncomfortable that's to say

what I can take in small doses

better said that which one must

Depends tolerate every once in a while

well / sometimes / every morning

in reality matinee / cocktail hour / and night

is when he repeats that we

speak in "sing-song"

and to mock us he says "singy-songy"

do you pronounce it "sing-song" or "singy-songy?"

I say independently of how we speak

(R. Dalton) do you say "singy-songy" or "sing-song?"

I didn't think so.

why bother

to talk about how she got here
with an outstretched hand
like she didn't know how to buy
to flush the toilet asking me
misses carmen this
misses carmen that
—don't call me misses!
is what I told her
call me carmen
but not "*cam-men*" like you say it

would you believe me she acted offended.

what I can't rid her of is that "s"

alberto cabero & juan bautista alberdi s.a.

for years the press has been asking in every possible way that the government start preventing the entrance into national territory of such people that, far from bringing the most minimal tendency towards work or action, represent a true social danger. It is already known that Gypsies live off thievery, swindling, and any illegal means, since they don't practice honorable work. Their arrival to a port always coincides with worsening delinquency, the disappearance of children, etc., etc. The government knows all the circumstances. Furthermore, the government knows that in other countries, even in neighboring states, they have already taken action against social riffraff. But the government, our leaders, persist in their impassivity, whether out of a spirit of hospitality or as apathy. Meanwhile, the Gypsies, the Chinese, the seditious by trade, the pimps, the outlaws, in short the dregs of society, move freely among us and feel at home. We are magnanimous to a fault.

Says it's not the brown skin it's not the umber and
it's not enough
To say it for the arrival gets upset or pale
Convinces himself that the adjective is a euphemism of disdain
It's the same in Upper Volta they say almost like a
hazelnut.

But when he sleeps the monster escapes him
At his side his snow-white wife begs him
Not to lie when he walks on his two paws

That if he drowns if he kills the den it would return
with fervor
To bite what he cannot
To caress what spills forth

Says it's not the curry through the stinking skin and
it's not enough
to say it for the one who stays
Breathes dreams
That his eye finally opens.

well, well

this really caught on
it's like it will sweep up
everything in its path
the well, well
like a teutonic butcher
whoa/ already started with her
well, well same as the
umm, umm, umm, because
have you heard the umm, umm
uglier than the well, well?
poorer than the anyways, anyways
some show up with the Uruguayan ta/ latest
stylish sort/ buddy
—it's a problem of manners
—values are what's important
—depen depen depends a lot on the person.

marta ferrusola's aleya

for verena stolcke

... illiterate
Behind only the book that falls in the drain pipe
Leaving the blessing halfway in the sewer.

like
The foot sore from the very first step
Wants neither path nor shelter only kick.

the
And here where they see her cross her dry skin
Or make her circle of parasites laugh.

Arab
Wearily she boards the car that herds her
To the shed that gathers the ceased.

neighbors
She doesn't fester just wants to break her thirst
to sweep down and swiftly unravel her dreams
: That she wanders El Ejido crying out for a sign
: That her verses are being burned in the streets

(such
A synthetic bear hugs her
A bandage covers her stitches

a lamentable
Someone passes out some blankets

Someone mixes powdered juice.

caste) ...
Would you like to now add that she has died?

(G. Mistral)
(You can now add
    that she has died).

AG

practically

have to subtitle the *help*

—and that Jano went to Madona
(Mister Alejandro went to McDonald's)

—they'll have Media Culpa on soon
(in a few moments the television will show the program,
 "Mea Culpa")

—the brine is ready for her
(I just finished cleaning the blinds)

—the gentleman is a lazy pig
(my husband is useless)

—with the minimum she pays, nowhere to go or to stay
(with the salary that I pay her she doesn't have enough to send to
 her family let alone live here).

Domeyko & Pim Fortuyn

The trees on the avenue are big abandoned brooms
(Claude Lévi-Strauss)

Whoever wants to can go back
Alone or with your whole pack of thugs
Go on to your stinking avenues
                                        and dead meat
That someone looked at him
                                    that another exploited him
That the shadow on the sidewalk
                                        did not cover him.

You want to dance with the pretty one?
There aren't enough here?

This is how the pig gives thanks
When he ransacks the watermelon patch.

the other

that sticks to her
is like dirt
and it's not in their make up
it's not that she's
inherently disgusting
I mean she's mixed but not
that tainted
here the same thing happens
not being filthy
always looking as if
they wash in the canal
the proverbial problem of the race

—and the things their parents have instilled in them

—what I call "personal hygiene"

—yesssss. PER - SON - AL - HY - GI - ENE.

AJ

He Is Just Beating His Flesh

He Is Just Beating His FleshSERNAM-AfganistaM

how many loaves are in the oven?

—Twenty-one burned!   "did you mean:

—Who burned them?

how many countries

WHO BURNED THEM?

are in the oven?"

WHO BURNED THEM?

WHO BURNED THEM?   (Google).

mossi, understand

for modou kara faye
antonio méndez rubio & enrique falcón

Language is a virus that comes from space
Language is a virus that comes from your hunger
Language is a virus that comes from cowardice.

Language is a virus that comes from your melancholy
Language is a virus that comes from the colostrum
Language is a virus that comes from bone dust

Language is a virus that comes from lovers
Language is a virus that comes from phlegm
Language is a virus that comes from your grainfield.

Language is a virus that comes from the trachea
Language is a virus that comes from fever
Language is a virus that comes from the torch

Language is a virus that comes from teardrops
Language is a virus that comes from your bile
Language is a virus that comes from urea.

Language is a virus that comes from nerves
Language is a virus that comes from ataxia
Language is a virus that comes from death.

Language is a virus that comes from your death
Language is a virus that comes from your cancer
Language is a virus that comes from your coldness.

Language is coming that is a virus of the silent.

AM

guild

for claudio b. & carles feixa

I went to Morgan and told him:
give me my portrait you have in your head.
"Don't get mad," he told me,
"take it."
He opened his head and gave it to me.
Afterwards I went to Taylor:
Edward, my portrait you have in your head
give it to me
"You are sick," he said
I lost patience and struck him
opened his skull and removed my portrait.

Boas heard the shouting and came running:
but my son, what have you done?
Another victim fell
I opened him up and removed my portrait.

Mead visited me:
Maggie give me my portrait you have in your head.
She opened her skull and gave it to me.
I looked for Ruth and silently
opened her skull with a crowbar
removed my photograph blaspheming
With her skull open
Open as I left the door to her house.

(Evans happened by
With his own rifle I blew his brains out seizing my image)

I returned and everyone was there having lunch

Claude L.-S. and the Pole
Got up and without even saying hello
opened both of their seminal skulls and gave me the portrait
saluting me.

I left and went to my "friends."

Word had traveled and I had no problem
They greeted me amiably
While with the other hand they gave me my portrait
"Thank you," I told them at the same time
And I closed their skulls with deference.

On the seventh day I went to No Where
With my leather and wool bag rife with photos
I stood on my toes as high as I could
And put them on top of a passing cloud and set them on fire.

I returned swiftly
I looked for my friends one by one

But they were all there

With yet another portrait of me in their head.

I'd want the Arabs to

sweep in once again.

Hitler's biggest mistake

was not having destroyed

Paris. The only thing

that humanity would

have appreciated, the one

good memory he could

have left behind he didn't,

leave, he didn't do it.

Why? Because the Ger-

man soldiers got lost

in the Metro.

(N. Perlongher)

I went around snooping among the Blacks
I had whiskey
in the hammock but longed for ice
Afterwards I went to get my suit dirty
And determined that everything functions
according
to its parts
That they are mortals
and their legs reach the ground.

I tried to win a few over
With the excuse that I was studying
Their strange way of moving their lips.

They taught me to bark like they barked
I translated a pair of their stories
A random poem.

I went to Oxford
I somehow became a doctor
They accused me of plagiarizing
Of lying about their rocks
Of not eating their food

I suffered I was poor
And I had to sell knowledge

What tall tales what destitution
But you already know
I am working on a little book where I relate
all of this.

teophrastus

"One of the few genuinely historical books written by an anthropologist *de carrière* is my own book."
(Evans-Pritchard).

The first desire that awakens in a traveler who discovers himself in a village where he hasn't been is to walk through the streets to judge their physical look and satisfy his natural curiosity. This was, then, the first rite that the country-folk practiced upon their arrival to Santiago. Before setting out on their way they took in all the signs of the inn, to find it in case they felt like getting lost. Accustomed to walking through the middle of the street in their land, they walked on the outside of the sidewalk, in a line, one by one, pacing back and forth. Sometimes they fell flat on their faces in some pile of trash, others plunged their feet into some sewer, others were pushed by some porter or broke their noses against some scaffolding. The carriages, of course, were empty, because, seeing them come, they tore off like souls possessed by the devil. (...) Indispensably they had to carry something with them, because they had no idea what to do with their idle hands. To this end, the first thing they bought was a walking stick with a rapier and a silver watch that they took out from block to block. (...) At the table they mistook everything: they slurped the roasted eggs from their hands, and put the shell in the cup; they ate ice cream with bread, and wolfed down candy with the wrapper. They resorted to fisticuffs anytime the server brought them a bill. (...) They asked first for the price of anything they wanted to buy in a store; they made the storekeeper take everything down and then put it back up, unfold and fold the items. When things were more than a peso, they complained of a lack of money and invariably asked for a discount. To end the disagreement they proposed to split the difference so it wouldn't be what either one said. A freebie "throw in a little extra, don't be a miser," were the last words of every purchase. They entered the costume store to ask for lighters, links, paper cuts, flint rocks, scented soaps, stamps of saints, bells for their cats. Not finding any of these articles, they said "in Santiago no one sells anything." (Pedro Ruiz Aldea)

carefully responds "well said" when you insult him. makes faces when you tell him about the death of your mother and spits on the floor you polished. claims to have read the books stolen from you and predicts the death of your dog after a long battle with an illness. is proud that he intercedes for you and never stops interceding for you and will never stop interceding for you so they don't give you a double shift. and writes a memo where he accuses you of wasting time organizing fraudulent "campaigns of excess." invites you to coffee to clear up that he confused the z of your name and accused the wrong person. swears he will make amends for his mistake and justice will be served and that he wants to kill himself. a bit later bursts into laughter among your peers describing your face with his "spontaneous" joke. asks for more time. and doesn't stop talking about the distinct concep-tions of time.   and of being named hernán soruco cardemil.

one from there

will summon you to useless meetings to inscribe herself in your calendar. to inscribe herself in the calendars of your few friends. to inscribe herself in the calendars of anyone who can get her the spotlight. will say the south is slow. that they don't know kitano they don't read yehuda amichai that there isn't a bío-bío bazaar. will call to ask you for numbers, will never cease asking you for numbers. will apply will win will forget you. will get an alcohol license through your friends. a central location. will sell. will restore Thai food. will hire illegally. will appear in the local regional national newspaper next to The Gem to Avoid. will say the city is slow. that the hardware stores raise prices that the plaza fills up with pharmacies that they don't support small business. particularly the exotic restoration. because there is nothing to eat because the avocados arrive soft because they sell humitas in the street. that she can't bear it. how happy a month in the summer and afterwards back from where she never should have left. and she doesn't go. still prospers more. has many employees. opened her own sector of lingerie shoe and grocery stores. becomes a member of the auction houses. solicits and tosses aside support. wants a plot of land. wants a subdivision. wants "something" facing the river. accuses them of not inviting her. that she is bored. that her cocktail is squalid.   that she wants to choose authority.

another from here

never gets up to clear his plate. speaks poorly of your wife and asks for wine. wants a "good" knife and tells you where you should buy meat. doesn't like the lamb anymore. doesn't like the short ribs anymore. keeps putting his foot on your flowerpot. argues against the weeds the gorse the pigs. offers you wire and a boat maker. explains to you at length why you know nothing about fruit trees. why you shouldn't fill yourself up on hazelnuts why your children look skinny. is reading the "ethnologists" but the war novel is better. calls at two asking you for a mechanic. asks that you repeat the name of your town to bring it up with his mother. repeats a story where you felt like a disgrace. calls at two to invite you to bingo. greets your wife with a hug. sings to her tells her stories makes sure to ask for her sister. for wine.   for her tragedy.

the ones from here [alfredo lefebvre]

delegate everything. say: little man take care of this. when you have a moment call him. take care of it I'm leaving at twelve fifteen. noooo it's so simple. it's a matter of meeting and explaining it to him. he wants three estimates. decide nothing make a lot travel too much. their coffee breaks are long. their meetings serious. get drunk talking like the neighborhood municipal leaders of management. detail what they do. the institutional goals the criticism they have for the few well-oiled productive cogs. ask you for a tiny little favor when they can. that you write this down, that you make sure, that you let them know, that some letters came, that something was left pending.   that "you represent us."

exaggerates. deepens his voice and declares and presents. a case he says is emblematic. his argument moves along and he interrupts himself with a joke. generally undecipherable. generally offensive. babbles dribbles dubs. raises his tone manages to make himself understood asks forgiveness for his insistence. contributes sentences like "it doesn't mean you can't celebrate it." "the hen is the strategy of the egg to make more eggs." uses commas when it's a matter of style. his anxiety makes him gain weight. imitates the cashier when talking to the cashier. nothing occurs to him but to buy nuts to go to the doctor for his gastritis. for his sebaceous problems for his bruxism. wants to wear glasses and doesn't need them. asks to speak and mistakenly cites george simmel cites germán arestizabal. they don't pay attention to him. explains his problems with epistemological paradigms that he hasn't translated well. calls attention to himself. gets them to follow his prolonged and off the cuff idea that he refuses to elaborate for confidentiality for lack of bibliography. for lack of good libraries for lack of good editors for lack of good researchers for lack of nightspots. at chamber concerts he sings along bangs on the seat in front. with his foot with the program with his keychain. they pick him for insignificant committees. what culture what expanse what DEYSE operation. accepts. they give him a movie ticket.   he misplaces it.

a troublemaker

to fear. crazy for handbags. of lupita ferrer ubiquity. prepares consommé. snacks to go. overdoes her makeup shouting. overwhelms herself contemplating. overstates herself investigating. fails the socialite exam. but licks what she has to lick. looks for a box seat. worse: a social-climber to fear. her tones are high her heels are high. cries out over nothing interrupts for everything. elbows. cuts in line. inserts herself. offers herself to organize to segregate to reappear to restructure to patronize.   give her power.

the theoretical one

professor from birmingham professor from mehuín huape puringue poor professor from frankfurt relocated in '33 in columbia university professor from palo alto working on teja island pondering whether to quit the mental research institute professor from constanza with airs of a housing debtor partly active in the vienna circle in the yale group appalls his thesis student with obvious attributions from the prague linguistic circle professor who doesn't answer about the mediums or the mediations that he paid no mind to the tel quel school and the ardener circle professor permeated by material it's that there is a lot of material it's that at some point he began to talk of the french annals school professor with serious discrepancies with the model of assisted suicide by retirement professor that talks of the advanced scene as if he spoke of his sick grandmother focuses the view on toothpaste tubes in glossy paper in the orfeo magazine and the santiago school getting laughs with the classic joke about the "nail" names only to land on the national & regional reality positioning himself more in italian micro history but they skewer him they ask him they criticize him they make his life hell people above all from río negro students in their majority of the population manuel rodríguez native alumnus from huelquén that lives in lanco that has come to study a major that serves for something that they are paying their scholarships under the impression to learn learning that is to say professor MAKING the finest mincemeat of reform and the reality that there is not a single mainstream chilean that at best the quito school and cuzco school name maybe a jorge millas to a h. matucana that no one tells him that he doesn't know more than he knows but the main role they suggest him for next year for the second event that they put in the program because they don't give credit to the cities here and the words "theoretical-practical" and "applied to." passionate professor. paralyzed professor.   scraped from god.

palacios navarro

there is nothing among the pillars of humanity more nefarious than the ambulant metic. passing for a stranger and recognized because of the "authentic" merchandise he carries at a lower price and if it's all just an obol tries everything to swap it for a dracma. he is always hungry and exploits his accent to inspire pity and procure salted meat in the market. he tests patience and his mendicant exclamations fill the alleyways. the ambulant will say: sir, do you need a ceedee, a nicktie, a horra movie. meanwhile others from his caste walk around with giant mutt bitches playing plebeian flutes. if you pass by without buying they will whisper behind your back that you are a stingy piece of shit and if you send them to be whipped they offer themselves to you as slaves underneath their stockings from almeria.

will do fieldwork will say they will love it will say he builds theory from the ground-up will say that to feel is patrimonial that he has discovered the theorem of rural winter tourism that he puts birds to sleep with a finger that he will see to it that the dogs learn sustainability. by the Atacama transport before the council before the mayor that the important thing isn't obsequiousness that what's vital is the synergy to be a quaver an endogenous power one more of the hydroponic relatives looks delighted when he is greeted will gain a position in planification will compound everything with local, local center, local network, local history, local capital they will offer him a course in geographic global positioning they will call him they will cite him the group the association the comission of the subcommittee of certitication. will whistle. will laugh.   will bury us.

artificial parasites

FROM: Human Resources
TO: All department heads █████ **and no** █████ **of the corporation**

O B J E C T I V E: <u>Put in place the norms for the correct use of Uniforms,
Security and Work Supplies</u>

The dispersal of Uniforms and Work Supplies represents a large human and financial burden for the
University, and as such it is helpful to establish some policies that assure the use of these items and
the standardization of their use. These items are listed below:

a) Uniform Use for Secretaries (Level G) and Administrators (Level F)

DIAS	DAMAS	VARONES
Monday	2002 Uniform (pink blouse)	2002 Uniform
Tuesday	2001 Uniform (light blue blouse)	2001 Uniform
Wednesday	2002 Uniform (patterned blouse)	2002 Uniform
Thursday	2001 Uniform (apricot or light blue blouse)	2001 Uniform
Friday	2002 Uniform (pink blouse)	2002 Uniform
	• Official University Activities: 2002 Uniform (patterned blouse) • We ask that you avoid wearing other items that do not correspond with assigned uniforms.	• The uniform can only be used with different shirts, according to the assigned uniform. All other garments must follow the above schedule.

b) All day and night Security Guards must use their uniform on a daily basis.

c. Remaining employees must be supervised in order to ensure the correct use of work and
security supplies provided by this department.

We hope that all employees will comply with these norms and we call on the department heads to
oversee the appropriate implementation of these regulations.

Sincerely,

████████████

DIRECTOR OF PERSONNEL

BD

this is a big hit with the kids

horizontal
business

What could be wrong with a woman with a song. *
Luis Vulliamy

* for Pao

because

whoever loves pays whoever cries brays
and alone alleviates and apprehends.

because whoever digs suffers whoever passes shifts
pitch amnion skips.

because whoever levitates licks whoever harms steeps
suite scrapes seethes.

because whoever flees captures whoever poses spoils
leg layer laurel.

because whoever prevents circumvents whoever seals reveals
cross cubby coxa.

because whoever gropes lies whoever spits pisses
must maize mixes.

because whoever grazes stays whoever closes latches.

there isn't

anyone that brings you this. a misfortune of honey and bee.
a door that seals any return.
and when it falls when it ricochets.
another sad sheet left white
folded for you in the insecurity.

then this feeble pain that looks for signs
this notch of scent in the concrete.

no one is left.
in the city only specters with a fleshy taste
that cannot sustain this message.
a telegram that pools
in a strange hallway perfume.

you will have to extend this hand towards yourself.
nothing is left
only this damp flare that dilates
a net of patchwork skin.
a bit of oil in the lip's articulations.
wax stains for the edges of your page.

That each time one is more alone on each side of the face . The prongs of the plug crackle . They make a *ziiich* while spitting two bursts of power . And that you don't want to go to any building that you want a dog . But you don't dare to listen to barking . That they remind you of the light switch from your dwelling. *Woof-woof* scratching your eyebrow with a cold teaspoon . You open an eyelid and you plead it doesn't match the other . This vision this bare cloud whose stench sews up your testicles . You want to hear everyone reading poetry . To keep on mocking yourself that you already always take salt baths . From sea With salt from there with fatal salt . With salt just so but you Don't want . You have never wanted to blow lint from the belly button . And to finish the rest of the soup you have left . And the other eyelid matches: it's the same: The box full of books and shoes and A Box Full of Books and Shoes . It's a splinter an eyelash a weight . You don't dare you don't want to go to the bathroom . You only want to play *pac-man* eating play-dough . But in front of a knife a fork a spoon . *Brag-Brag-Brag-brag* you are the young boy you The invitee the face on the bill that you pay with The one who takes the drinks off the truck the one who drives You the one that prints the dispatch guide. You want to leave You want to interview yourself to not hear yourself talk more nonsense . Stand up for yourself when you can insist on standing up for yourself Untie yourself from this delicate fetal position Unparalyze yourself Exercise the long arm playing some bells But you don't want to your feet hurt your shoelaces hurt . They don't make shoelaces like they used to Like they were to stop the blood and tie up the flow It's that you are the maker *il miglior fabbro* And you only wait until twelve at night to tell someone I'm Tired I'm hungry and there's Larkin clearly Larkin's there who tells you only the young can be alone freely and it doesn't fit because you are not a Verbal God you are an old cyst that stuffs itself that spreads in your exhausted tear duct And you should emerge from the amnion but you can't quite . You don't know how to stretch the fingers you have broken nails you have a broken life and a deflated neck And you want a pity suction a scrape a win Three pronged plugs bother you the color of the flame in the kitchen the distance between each line on the floor tile the tangle of the telephone cord your ankle You don't look You don't search for the precipice of the bed Only your legs are there the crumbs and your sheets The hard crumbs comfort your back the smell that your hair gives the blanket . You have yourself cornered curled up in the blades of a blender Waiting for the ice the water the sugar Waiting for someone to come and turn it on You just want them to turn it on AND blend you AND drink you and not furrow their brow and pee you out and have you do something for the hazelnut tree that is dying . But No . The plug . They are the prongs of the plug that don't go in . It won't Start . You are there entombed inside the juicer . *brrr* . cold . alone . The hair with seeds . hard. transparent . Waiting . between the cubes Awaiting twelve at night to tell someone that it is twelve at night.

nnn

(No one fears
plaque
mud
or the stench of the teapot.

Nor that the semen rots
in the bathing suit.

And you can invite your friends
To close

Finally
From the outside).

thought I had conquered the spiders
that long ago
amassed in front of the jars of spice and jelly
but they keep circling and trapping
tiny deformed insects that seek nothing
but to die with light in the window.

I sprayed insecticide
to catch them when they crawl towards the cupboard

"I want you to aid me in this struggle
they are more like you," I told her

yes. it was close to 13 thirty. there was no boiled water
nor sugar to mix in the teacups.
"you are an anti-environmental piece of shit," she yelled at me
everythingyoudototheenvironmentitwilldobacktoyou
yes. there wasn't a refrigerator there wasn't a bed
nor the pillow that I stuffed long ago
of the curtains I also remember nothing.

at my side two or three boxes with opaque objects
and the spiders that waited for me in that grimy glass
in that empty cave.

the nails were tight in the wood
the wind moved other bits of wind
the door still balanced on the hinges
the water left the faucet for the drain
the flies did ample figure eights
the light bulbs asphyxiating in the sockets
but the spiders
the spiders kept coming and going.

"in conclusion this is my life," she said

parting huge mouthfuls of smoke with a tick of her arm.

I sensed something of the perverse and bitter.

This is my life and she said in passing

that the umbilical we were sharing

held history food terror and dense confusions

made us two beings

swept along by distinct gravities.

"This is my life," she said

saying this blanket this glass this abyss this wound that time contains and expands. Wanting to say you do not want this immense marvel that bleeds. you go overboard looking for a body between your nose. you have remained at the table for one. OK. I wanted to excuse myself

but she grabbed the neck of the balloon that held me down.

gave it her usual salty shove.

turned on the radio.

touched it with a thorn.

when

finally I could wake up/ I had on the edge
of the bed the girl I never
spoke to at the bar to not get into problems with
my patch of rancor

she brandished shorts and the frizzy hair falling over her face.
she brought a glass of yogurt and a piece of peach without skin without imperfections in a
cup with spotted dalmatians
the clock was off and by the wind it could have been perfectly
7 in the evening.

I was ashamed/ covered from head to urethra
with that stiff corset that refuses the kiss of the flat teat.

the room smelled of beasts and kilos of dead clothes were strewn about.
I can't believe you are here
don't do this for my defeat —I mumbled
I can stand up myself and gather maqui and apples outside and tell you of some
trips to the underworld and back
(on the edge of the bed she was a green well a waterfall)

—I can still fry an egg

she passed a damp cloth over my cheeks and dislodged stains
that I was saving for several months and that had formed a weak coating
in perpetual expansion

you are clean —she whispered
stay to wait for the wind to pass stay to heal my bronchial tubes just
stay to stare at the back
of this immobile page
—I answered

when I finally could wake up/ I had on the edge of the bed the girl from the bar
that I didn't speak to/ that closed a window that vanished
now
I alone tie a knot in the heart of my shoes.

mmm [waldo rojas]

to stephanie decante & pedro araya

I like when children cry. because they are carried away.

everyone

for edwin madrid & aleyda quevedo

wants that one return to normality
the curtains want that one
return to normality
the exhausting fatties want you
to return to normality ma'am
do you want me to return to normality?
even germán the dead keyboard begs
when will you pay the fee for the assembly of normality tell me
without circumlocution if you feel like it direct me
to the central office of normality to the file
to apply for normality ding dong bell
white normality's shift
brotha brotha come back through normality
do you fear me? he will say in quito the Middle of the Earth
address yourself, then, therefore, before, to normality
Word, seriously— Do you want this to be the path to normality?
It's personal but they will be calm but they'll be pleased
anyway tell me to my face if they'll stop
if tomorrow I come here and if tomorrow I come upon style
normality through being an aftertaste perhaps an air
I am about to convert today
I am about to become one
with normality.

[adrian henri]

Roger McGough
No. Even better another nun
Waiting to advance in
The movie line asking herself
How it would be to buy popcorn
For two.

from weighing, weigh

from weighing, weigh/ knick-knack or tacky rock/ weighs.
from brushing, brush/ altar/ colander/ rush
from filtering, fit/ fallacy or impostor/ flit
from standing, standup/ defense or forward/ standoff

from writing,

but let me finish

[Durruti]
Too Many Committees!

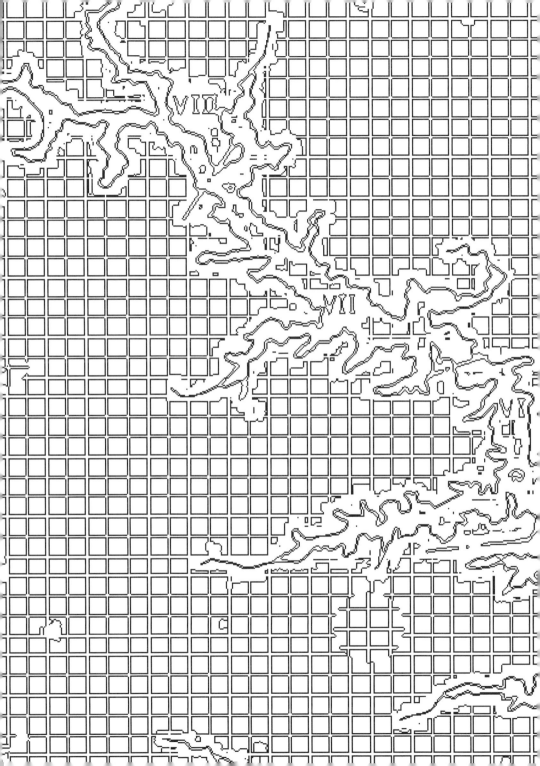

Alto Volta
Yanko González

Nace i su cuna de bronce se lo vende Busquets, Seckel, Lumsden; las ropas que lo abrigan las envía la casa Prat, la casa Francesa o la casa Escocesa; el coche lleno de juguetes en que lo pasea la English nurse, lo manda Krauss. Crece i los padres Franceses o el Instituto Inglés se encargan de su educación. Sus libros escolares se los vende Tesche, Ivenso Conrado. Su ropa se la hacen Pujol, Pinaud, Cerri, Delteil, Geue, Biagini, Serveau, Dufresne, Cornaglia, Falabella, Russo, Ouvrard o Casini; sus zapatos Pepay, Vuletich, Canguilhem, Rouxel, Werneburg, Ancich; su sombrero Launay, Cohé, capellaro, Voigt, La Joven Italia Wieger, Chopis, Wegener, Haudeville o Biaut. Sus pelotas para foot-ball o lawn-tennis, se las venden Diener, Hume o Melrose; sus cigarros se los venden Pabst, Silberstein, Wageman o Kähny; los licores Weir Scott, Stirling o Hayes. Deposita su plata en el Deutsche Bank, en el banco Italiano o en el banco español; su caja de fondos se la compra a Söhrens o a Bash; asegura su vida en la Equitable Life Assurance Co. O en la New York Life Assurance Co. I su casa en la Royal FIRE Assurance Co. O en la Lancashire Sure Co. Compra sus muebles a Elliot Rourk, a Bruhn a Giordano o a Muñecas. Sus alfombras se las vende Muzardhue i Fallay o La Riojana; sus cortinas Brecciani; su cocina Styles o Slutzki; las pailas i cacerolas Gleisner, Barabino, Dabadie, Limozin; sus lámparas Séller o Daneri; su baño, Morrison o Cucurull; las lozas Biancheri o Mondito; sus provisiones, Vacarezza, Castagneto, Capurro, Porcile, Rovano o Ramsay; su piano Kirsinger; Doggenweiler, o Golz; su coche Ledermann, Bardeua o Douzet; los arneses para sus caballos Coudeuu camalez, Liebe o Placier; su automóvil Coppeta o Tisné; sus medicinas Moutier, Fritz o Lebeuf; su reloj i prendedores Waak, Emmanuel, Weil und Becker; Müller, Hüber, Levy, Meylan, Gauret, Jacob, Umaluf, Köhler, Godart, Ghiringhell, Houluigue; sus corbatas Grote o Mattas; sus camisas Guillerat, Botín o Wanauld; sus guantes Mautier o Mèriot; su máquina de escribir Curlet o Chirwing; su plancha de abogado Chanalet, Boschaner, Depret o Texier. Compra sus cuadros donde Schlak, Dell'Orto o Strozzi; sus anteojos a Strautvetter o Eiter; los libros para su biblioteca a Nascimento o Baldrich; le empastan sus libros Dietsch o Schram. Su máquina fotográfica la compra a Hans Frey o Durandin; se corta el pelo i se afeita donde Jardel, Cantelli i Cascini o Brun; se hace fotografiar donde Spencer o Heffer; su luz eléctrica la instala Weber, Siemens und Schukert, Yahn o Raabellet; sube en los tranvías de la Chilean Electric Tranway and Light Co. Ltd.; sale en viaje i toma carros de la St. Louis Car Co.; aloja en el Royal Hotel o en el Hotel Ingles en Valparaíso; navega por nuestras costas en el Pacific Steam Navigation Co. Por último, si muere, le envian el ataud i lo trasladan a su última morada Boher o Forlivesi i su lápida mortuoria la hacen Ceppi o Botinelli con la inscripción latina Requiescat in pace. (Tancredo Pinochet Le-Brun).

ejemplo

Quieren que me vaya como si yo no quisiera irme
Entonces les digo me voy
Pero al primer
o quinto paso
Corren a buscarme
para que les planche el aire
Les abra una zanja
donde han de cruzar sus trajes.

En el atrio del pueblo hay
un ciruelo añoso,
Todas las primaveras
brotan renuevos:
Los pasaportes viejos no
pueden hacer eso, amada,
los pasaportes viejos no
pueden hacer eso.
(W. H. Auden)

Ayer fue lo mismo
Entendí claramente
quieren que me vaya
Eso es lo que se decían mientras cuidaba de sus niños
Yo jugaba a lo que en Alto Volta se jugaba
Ejemplo
La silla se llama lavabo la puerta sardina
La mesa vajilla y los zapatos *cadira*
Entonces los niños gritaban
Amarillo
Ábrenos la sardina.

Era un juego y dijeron que me fuera
Que tenía que enseñarles las palabras
Como se debían

Ejemplo
abrir la boca
se dice
reír.

venas por su sangre

venas por su sangre
tumores en la tarde.

tiene té falta fe.
su padre crece.

pregunta hola tú
si algo sobra si

hace hambre
quedará menú.

uñas de la madre
saliva por la tarde

pisará perú.

en cada país los vicios y los males universales de los hombres y de la sociedad humana se señalan como específicos del lugar. Yo nunca he estado en sitio donde no haya oído: aquí las mujeres son vanas e inconstantes, leen poco y están mal instruidas; aquí el público está pendiente de los asuntos ajenos, es muy charlatán y maldiciente; aquí el favor, la ruindad y el dinero lo pueden todo: aquí reina la envidia, y las amistades son poco sinceras, y así sucesivamente; como si en otros sitios las cosas se condujeran de otras manera. Los hombres son miserables por necesidad y están resueltos a creerse miserables por accidente. (Leopardi).

que no quiere

« Que
no
quiere
morir
como
un
perro
nadie
quiere
morir
como
un
perro
todo
ser
humano
merece
no
morir
como
un
perro
ha
vivido
como
cerdo
y
no
quiere
morir
como
un
perro ».

«vine a ver a
mis amigos»,
me oyeron
gritar por
teléfono
apretándome
con furia el
otro oído.
(e. dobry).

No,
si puedes quedarte
pero sucede
es decir la casa está
digamos que no hay
mucho por donde una
o dos puedan veamos
es que estoy con un ritmo
digo al mismo tiempo
con esto para allá
con lo otro preferiría
No,
si puedes quedarte
pero sucede
es decir la casa está
digamos que no hay
mucho por donde una
o dos puedan veamos
es que estoy con un ritmo
digo al mismo tiempo
con esto para allá
con lo otro preferiría
No,
si puedes quedarte
pero sucede
es decir la casa está
digamos que no hay
mucho por donde una
o dos puedan veamos
es que estoy con un ritmo
digo al mismo tiempo
con esto para allá
con lo otro preferiría
No,

L

lo que engrana

lo que engrana le impulsa y lo voltea
un ojo se cae al blanco mientras los de abajo
corren hacia un juego nuevo.
él los ha visto todos: planifica:
el que te deja boca arriba
el que te vomita la boquera
el que te grita la membrana
el averno de los campesinos la cavidad de los ancianos.

veo a mi madre que se toma de los fierros y no alcanza
veo a mi padre que fuma rápido leyendo precauciones
mi hermano me asesta un golpe en el estómago muy fuerte
mientras lo mancho con un palo de algodón dulce.

la felicidad ja ja ja ja cantan el dúo
que posa en una silla voladora
que me dio tu amor // hoy quiero cantar
me paso largo rato pensando por qué no nos reímos
mejor a eso no me subo.
festín final de los felices.

ahora queremos una bicicleta
mi hermano una pistera yo una *bici cross*
hemos sudado flema para llegar al parque
lejos más lejos que Alto Volta
mi padre dijo no fue sencillo
y carga de vuelta un oso grande.

pordentro&porfuera

O sea
estuvo muchos años extrayendo heces
aunque   vamos
todos le decíamos el saca-mierdas
que traducido a su idioma vendría a ser
ducha fría   o   saca-piedras.

Convengamos que la mierda es memoria
del mismo modo que una palabra
es la memoria de su significado
repetía haciéndose el interesante
abriendo o cerrando el peso de las naranjas
de anne michaels con dibujos de john berger.

Pero vamos
un Trabajo de Mierda
para colmo en negro como la mierda negra
cómo explicarlo en nuestra lengua
se podría traducir como
un trabajo «verdaderamente» ingrato.

Y aunque usaba un traje guantes máscara y un lindo
casco verde
hedía
por dentro y por fuera
de hecho yo fui el que le puse
el pordentro&porfuera que en nuestro idioma
significa algo así como
el fétido externo ensombrece al fétido interno
amalgamándose hasta la hediondez extrema.

El punto es que se pasó sus buenos años
absorbiendo aquello
y ya se sabe
aunque las moscas cambien
las piedras siempre serán las mismas.

Y de esas frases que soltaba
como para su redención futura
fue quedando un fatal cansancio obvio
automáticas palabras varilla sonda acople
llave inglesa papel residencia quizás quince.
Mucha mierda.

Publicó algo
y volvió al Alto Volta
pero olía mal
el «caca blanca» le apodó su familia
que viene a significar más o menos sin certeza
alejándose o acercándose al campo semántico
aquel que trabajó como poeta
para los que nos traen
o nos quitan el trigo
de la boca.

O sea.

heribert barrera

hay muchas maneras de hacer infelices a los hombres. una de ellas es visitándolos.

Cuando izamos la bandera se nos ocurrió que azar sirve también para llegar
No decir que esto acababa mal que a tus amigos se les ha caído el corazón
que no es verdadero eso de lo único verdadero: *un jour j'aurai dit oui à ma naissance*

Sabes cuando la izamos vimos a través (que ya es suficiente *Québécois* para llegar)
Detrás los mismos ríos la misma amoratada amortajada con los ojos abajo realidad
Los párpados pisados y un alfabeto duro astillado para la lengua para entrar

Padre no quiso izar y arrancó un pedazo de su pierna para no salir para entrar
Dijo el sur lo que se ha de ablandar lo que se ha de caer lo que había que morir
Pero estaba afuera y veloz paseaba su voltaje entre los átomos de aire. Pobre.

Al cubrir que es el morir lo volcamos al pie del mástil no podíamos fijar el iris la pestaña
No era nadie en particular que la bruma se tragaba no era nadie un padre triste
Triste. Triste como un padre muerto triste al pie de un mástil izando bandera triste.

marsellesa

primera estrofa integrar para colocarla becar para modularla consolar para alterarla segunda estrofa ofrecerle para buscarle entenderle para trabajarle confundirle para traducirle tercera estrofa censarte para regalarte aprenderte para correrte refugiarte para televisarte cuarta estrofa comprarlo para introducirlo premiarlo para permitirlo quinta estrofa para explotarlo para expatriarlo para expoliarlo sexta estrofa.

paralosalemanesesinclusobuenoquelaspalabrasseanalgo
largas, puescomosontardosdepensamiento, asídisponende
tiempopararefexionar.

Qué poca honradez hay entre los escritores. Se hace patente
en la desvergüenza con que falsean sus citas de escritos
ajenos. Pasajes de mis obras los encuentro completamente
desfgurados (…).

Los franceses, incluidas las Academias, dan a la lengua
griega un trato ultrajante. Toman de ella palabras para desf-
gurarlas: escriben, por ejemplo, *etiologie, esthétique* (…),
o también *Oedipe, Andromaque,* etc.; es decir, escriben las
palabras griegas tal y como lo haría un gañán francés que
las hubiese oído pronunciar a otros. (…) Ver maltratada
la lengua griega a favor de una jerga tan repugnante como
es de suyo la francesa (este italiano echado a perder de la
manera más repugnante, con las largas y repulsivas sílabas
finales y el sonido nasal) es un espectáculo comparable al
que ofrece una araña de las Indias Occidentales cuando se
come un colibrí, o un sapo cuando engulle a una mariposa.

Qué poca honradez hay entre los escritores. Se hace patente
en la desvergüenza con que falsean sus citas de escritos
ajenos. Pasajes de mis obras los encuentro completamente
desfgurados (…).

la belleza es griega. pero la conciencia de que sea griega es chilena.
nada es, todo se otrea.

T

deja

a juan pablo gómez

deja constancia en carabineros. resuelve poniendo una constancia en carabineros. afecte lo que le afecte dice yo soy de los que pongo una constancia en carabineros. si sucede algo si me vulneran. si me molestan por el idioma. no, no. dejo constancia en carabineros. que no cuesta nada quedas tranquilo dice un trámite más un trámite menos. ilustra con su sobrina en pittsburgh con su vecino en lleida. sin abogados sin leguleyos poniendo constancia en carabineros. que si va a mayores. que si se pone negro. que a uno lo dejan en la frontera recomienda la debida constancia en carabineros. en su experiencia nunca hay cola. ni en matucana ni en países de todas partes. que se espera en la guardia que se solicita soy de afuera y vengo a instalar una constancia en carabineros. y que vale la pena te buscan pieza. piensa que se trata de tomarle el peso. después solo después buscar trabajo. vendiendo humo. pero devuelve. pero repite de no hacer tal. de no pasar. de no dejarse estar. de no estampar lo que decía de carabineros.

U

baldar

Cuando se arrastra se nos permite decir «Ya Casi Yace»
Que no tiene capacidad que no dice no al pan que lo repleta
Y se le sigue dando abriéndolo hinchándolo
Lisiando su capacidad motora

Pavo en Navidad.

mercat de las flores

a martín g. & pablo méndez

en el asiento de adelante: los gambarotta, en el de atrás: los gonzález. sin ser ninguno
de los dos iba tirado atrás

haciéndose por último el gonzález.

Señores pasajeros, me subo a esta

al bajarse en el bareto, por marroca pelo rizo ojera ancha

micro a ganarme la vida porque no

le insultan le mentan el coño la madre.

tengo trabajo, y no tengo trabajo

disimula, sigue sin más silbando por su marcha.

porque no cumplo con los siguientes

pero por dentro está muriendo

requisitos: no soy peruano; ten-

O QUÉ PENSABAS.

go rasgos caucásicos y no morenos;

mido un metro noventa y no un

metro cincuenta (…) (Aedo).

W

onofre lindsay

Fotografiarnos y vernos en movimiento en su pequeña pantalla gigante
Una buena idea para quien gusta de su doble más que su esperpento
Quien se husmea y le harta la acidez de sus tres pares de axilas
Idea buena idea para quienes se blanquean.

Algo así como un *Voyeur* de las encías
Un Fisgón ocular del globo

Boya de ocasión para fantasmas.

jefa de vegetales

siendo cajera en el HIPER me ascendieron a jefa de
vegetales por esa manera exacta de devolver el vuelto
esa habilidad sin trámite de sacar galana
la melona golpeada/ la vinagre mugrienta.

quieta habilidad de encontrar callada
en la malla de kilo la papa blanda
esa vergüenza de la yagana
así con la uña larga/ rompía el hilo rajaba el ato
y echaba a la zanahoria palta la lechuga lenta.

qué cirugía fina/ qué odontología/
 p e r o q u é s i n t o n í a
pero haberme visto/ QUÉ CALIGRAFÍA.

los chilenitos no entendían los reponedores
 me jodían
si en Neuquén no crece nada si la sidra la revuelven
con el gas de cañería.
pero cho/ pero yo/ seguía/
la guerra del desierto
la jefa de vegetales de la pampa perdida
llenando mi canasto de fruta podrida.

qué tersura/ qué pasillo/ qué chacra hermosa
la de esta zorra argentina
que le quitó el laburo
al chilote de la fiambrería

qué ricura/ qué heroína
que acusó de hurto
al mapuche de la
panadería.

Y

El que pasea se solaza de su imagen que proyecta la vidriera
No sabe que no es él lo que el cristal devuelve
Que la transparencia no fija su líquida figura

todas las lenguas extranjeras

Pero insiste en posar para una foto interminable
Componiendo para sí lo que el parto no produjo
Balanceando la carne de un pie a otro
Negando con la córnea sus fisuras.

me inspiran un sagrado rencor.

Como si no bastara con la luz que no coincide
Mueve su cabeza al dial que le acomoda
Pero el mensaje que en sordina la radio expande
Es la efigie: misma imagen misma voz
Que su propio mandamás soslaya.

(E. Lihn)

pero ponte en mi lugar pero
es que ponte en mi lugar es
lo que te digo ponte en mi
lugar encuentras justo que
no se ponga en mi lugar y
me pida a mí solamente que
haga el esfuerzo de ponerme
en su lugar sin molestarse
siquiera en ponerse en mi
lugar y pedir y pedir y pedir
que sólo se pongan en su lugar
dios mío que lío *quien fuera
blanco aunque fuese catalán*.

es que

a coke z. & carolina o.

¿Chile...? te grita / no te habla / no
lo habíamos comentado
a
es que es cierto / no es el acento
ya le hubiéramos dicho
lo que me incomoda es decir
lo que soporto a medias
más bien lo que hay que
Depende tolerar de vez en cuando
bueno / a veces / todas las mañanas
en realidad matiné / vermut / y noche
es cuando repite que nosotros
hablamos cantadito
y para humillarnos dice «cantaíto»
¿tú pronuncias «cantadito» o «cantaíto»?
digo independiente de que hablemos así
(R. Dalton) ¿tú dices «cantaíto» o «cantadito»?

yo no encuentro.

para qué

hablar de cómo llegó aquí
con una mano adelante
si no sabía comprar
para tirar la cadena me preguntaba
señora carmen esto
señora carmen esto otro
— no me digas señora !
fue que le dije
dime carmen
pero no «*cam-men*» como te sale.

me creerás que se hizo la ofendida.

lo que no le he podido quitar es la ese

alberto cabero & juan bautista alberdi s.a.

hace ya años que la prensa viene pidiendo en todos los tonos que el gobierno proceda a impedir la entrada al territorio nacional de semejante jente que, lejos de traer el mas nimio continjente del trabajo o de accion, encarnan un verdadero peligro social. Ya se sabe que los jitanos viven de la rateria, del embauque o de cualquier otro medio vedado, pues el trabajo honrado no lo practican. Su llegada a un puerto coincide siempre con el recrudecimiento de la delincuencia, con las desapariciones de niños, etc., etc. El gobierno conoce todas estas circunstancias. El gobierno conoce, ademas, que en otros paises, aun en los que son nuestros vecinos, ya se ha procedido en contra de esta morralla social. Pero el gobierno, nuestros dirigentes, continuan en su impasibilidad, ignoramos si por espíritu hospitalario o por decidía. Entre tanto los jitanos, los chinos, los sediciosos de oficio, los tratantes de blancas, los perseguidos, en fin toda la hez de la sociedad, afluye a nosotros y se siente aqui como en su casa. Somos magnánimos hasta la exajeración.

Dice no es la piel morena no es la tostadura y no consigue
Con decirlo que el que llega se inmute o palidezca
Se convenza que el adjetivo sea un eufemismo del desdén
Es igual en Alto Volta dicen casi igual que una avellana.

Pero al dormir el monstruo se le escapa
A su lado su mujer semilla blanca le suplica
Que no mienta cuando camina en sus dos patas
Que si asfixia que si mata al cubil vuelva con ganas
A morder lo que no puede
Acariciar lo que derrama.

Dice no es el curry por la piel hedionda y no consigue
con decirlo que el que queda
Respire sueñe
Que su ojo por fin se abra.

ya, ya

eso se le pegó
es como si se quebrara
a todo le busca
el ya, ya
como carnicera teutona
uy/ ya empezó con su
ya, ya al modo de
amm, amm, amm, porque
has escuchado el amm, amm
más feo que el ya, ya?
más pobre que el endeque, endeque
algunos vienen con un ta uruguayo/ último
tipo tío/ hacere
— es asunto de educación
— lo importante son los valores
— depen depen depende mucho de la persona.

AF

aleya de marta ferrusola

a verena stolcke

... analfabeto
Atrás sólo el libro que cae a la atarjea
Dejando la oración a mitad del sumidero.

como
El pie llagado a partir del paso
No quiere camino ni posada sólo coz.

los
Y aquí donde le ven persigna su piel seca
O hace reír a los ácaros que le acompasan.

árabes
De reojo sube al carro que lo arrea
Al galpón que junta a los que cesan.

vecinos
No supura sólo quiere descansar la sed
Abatirse descoserse pronto lo que sueña

: Que vaga en El Ejido pidiendo una llamada
: Que le queman en la calle su versículo

(tan
Un oso sintético lo abraza
Una venda tapa la sutura

lamentable
Alguien reparte unas frazadas

Alguien revuelve un jugo en polvo.

casta) ...
¿Quisieran agregar ahora que se ha muerto?

(G. Mistral)
(Pueden agregar ahora
            que se ha muerto).

AG

prácticamente

a esta *china* hay que subtitularla:

— *y que Jano fue al Madona*
(don Alejandro fue al McDonald's)

— *ligerito dan Media Culpa*
(en unos momentos la televisión transmitirá el programa
 «Mea Culpa»)

— *le tengo listas las tercianas*
(acabo de finalizar la limpieza de las persianas)

— *el caballero es un cerdo a la izquierda*
(mi marido es un inútil)

— *con el mínimo que dá ni pallá ni pacá*
(con el sueldo que le pago no le alcanza para enviarle dinero a su
 familia ni para vivir aquí).

Domeyko & Pim Fortuyn

En la avenida los árboles son grandes escobas abandonadas
(Claude Lévi-Strauss)

El que desea pues que vuelva
Solo o entre una jauría de tunantes
Vayan a sus avenidas de hedor
                    y fiambre
Que alguien lo miró
              que el otro lo explotó
Que la sombra en la vereda
                no lo cobijó.

¿Quieren bailar con la bonita?
¿Acá no hay suficiente?

Así es como agradece el cerdo
Cuando el sandial revuelve.

AI

lo otro

que tiene pegado
es como piñén
y no es de fábrica
no es que originalmente
sea suciecita
o sea es cholita pero no
como barrosa
acá pasa lo mismo
no siendo cochinos
como que siempre pareciera
que se lavan en la acequia
el consabido problema de la raza

— y lo que le hayan inculcado lo padres

— lo que yo llamo «hábitos de higiene»

— eeeso. HÁ - BI - TOS - DE - HI - GIE - NE.

En Su Carne No Más Pega
En Su Carne No Más Pega SERNAM-AfganistáM

AK

¿cuántos panes hay en el horno?

— ¡Veintiún quemados! «quizás quiso decir:

— ¿Quien los quemó?

cuantos países

¿QUIEN LOS QUEMÓ?

hay en el horno»
¿QUIEN LOS QUEMÓ?

¿QUIEN LOS QUEMÓ? (Google).

AL

mossi, entiende

a modou kara faye
a. méndez rubio & e. falcón

El lenguaje es un virus que viene del espacio
El lenguaje es un virus que viene de tu hambre
El lenguaje es un virus que viene del cobarde.

El lenguaje es un virus que viene de tu pena
El lenguaje es un virus que viene del calostro
El lenguaje es un virus que viene de la cendra

El lenguaje es un virus que viene del que ama
El lenguaje es un virus que viene de la flema
El lenguaje es un virus que viene de tu serna.

El lenguaje es un virus que viene de la traquea
El lenguaje es un virus que viene de la fiebre
El lenguaje es un virus que viene de la tea

El lenguaje es un virus que viene de la lágrima
El lenguaje es un virus que viene de tu bilis
El lenguaje es un virus que viene de la urea.

El lenguaje es un virus que viene de los nervios
El lenguajes es un virus que viene de la ataxia
El lenguaje es un virus que viene de la muerte.

El lenguaje es un virus que viene de tu muerte
El lenguaje es un virus que viene de tu cáncer
El lenguaje es un virus que viene de tu frío.

El lenguaje viene que es un virus del que calla.

gremio

a claudio b. & carles feixa

Fui donde Morgan y le dije:
dame este retrato mío que tienes en la cabeza.
No te enojes –me dijo–
ya te lo doy.
Se abrió la testa y me lo dio.
Después fui donde Taylor :
Edward ese retrato mío que tienes en la cabeza
dámelo
Estás enfermo –dijo–
Me impacienté le di un palo
le abrí el cráneo y saqué mi retrato.

Boas escuchó el grito y vino corriendo:
pero hijo mío ¿qué has hecho?
Cayó otra víctima
Se lo abrí y saqué mi retrato.

Me visitó la Mead:
Maggie dame ese retrato mío que tienes en la cabeza.
Se abrió el cráneo y me lo dio.
Busqué a Ruth y mudo
le partí el cráneo con un fierro
le saqué mi fotografía blasfemando
Con el cráneo abierto
Como abierta le dejé la puerta de su casa.

(Se me cruzó Evans
Con su mismo rifle le destapé los sesos usurpándole mi imagen)

Volví y estaban todos almorzando

Claude L.-S. y el Polaco
Se levantaron y sin siquiera saludarme
se abrieron sendos cráneos y me dieron el retrato
haciéndome una venia.

Partí a donde todos mis «amigos».

Se había corrido la voz y no tuve ningún inconveniente
Me saludaban amablemente
Mientras con la otra mano me daban mi retrato
Yo les decía al mismo tiempo «gracias»
Y les cerraba su cráneo con deferencia.

Al séptimo día me fui a Ninguna Parte
Con mi bolso de cuero y lana repleto de fotografías
Me empiné como pude
Y las puse sobre una nube que pasaba y les prendí fuego.

Volví de una carrera
Los busqué uno por uno

Pero allí estaban todos

Con ese otro retrato mío en la cabeza.

ministerio

Yo querría que llegasen Anduve husmeando entre los Negros
Tenía whisky
los árabes de una pero en la hamaca deseaba un hielo
Después me fui a ensuciar el traje
vez por todas. El gran Y receté que todo funciona según los
elementos
error de Hitler fue no Que ellos son mortales
y las piernas les llegan hasta el suelo.
haber destruido París.
Le hice empeño a un par de cuantos
Lo único que la humanidad Con la excusa que estudiaba
Sus maneras raras de mover los labios.
le iba a agradecer, Me enseñaron a ladrar como ladraban
Les traduje un par de cuentos
el único buen Algún poema suelto.
recuerdo que podría Me fui a Oxford
Me hice doctor a todo esto
haber dejado no lo Me acusaron de plagiar
De mentir sobre sus piedras
dejó, no lo hizo. ¿Por De no comer sus alimentos
qué? Porque los soldados Padecía era pobre
Y tuve que vender conocimiento
alemanes se perdieron
Qué embustes qué miserias
en el Metro. Pero ustedes ya lo saben
Preparo un pequeño libro donde relato
(N. Perlongher) todo esto.

teofrasto

«Uno de los pocos libros genuinamente históricos escritos por un antropólogo *de carrière* es mi propio libro».
(Evans-Pritchard).

El primer deseo que se despierta en un viajero al hallarse en un pueblo que no conoce es el recorrer sus calles para juzgar de su aspecto físico y satisfacer su natural curiosidad. Esta era, pues, la primera diligencia que practicaban los provincianos al día inmediato de su llegada a Santiago. Antes de emprender su marcha tomaban todas las señas de la posada, para hallarla en caso de que se les antojara perderse. Acostumbrados a andar en su tierra por el medio de la calle, iban por fuera de las veredas, enfilados, de uno en uno, echando contrapasos atrás y adelante. Unas veces caían de bruces en algún rimero de basura, otras sumían sus piernas en alguna acequia, otras recibían el empuje de algún mozo de cordel o se rompían las narices contra algún andamio. De los carruajes sí que estaban libres, porque, viéndolos venir, arrancaban como alma que lleva el diablo. (…) Indispensablemente habían de llevar algo en las manos, porque teniéndolas desocupadas no sabían qué hacer con ellas. Para este efecto, lo primero que compraban era bastón con estoque y un reloj de plata, que iban sacando de cuadra en cuadra. (…) En la mesa todo lo equivocaban: los huevos asados se los sorbían en la mano, y la cáscara la ponían en la copa; los helados los tomaban con pan, y los dulces se los engullían con papel. Con los criados andaban a las puñadas cada vez que les pasaban la cuenta. (…) Para comprar algo en una tienda preguntaban primero por el precio de todo lo que veían; hacían subir y bajar al comerciante, doblar y desdoblar las piezas. Cuando la cantidad pasaba de un peso, se quejaban de la escasez de dinero y pedían indefectiblemente rebaja. Para terminar sus disputas proponían partir la diferencia para que no fuese lo que ambos decían. La yapa, «échele una larguita, no se corte usted las uñas», eran las últimas palabras con que cerraban sus compras. En las tiendas de fantasía se entraban a preguntar por mecheros, eslabones, hojas cortadas, piedras de chispa, jabón de olor, estampas de santos y cascabeles para los gatos. No hallando ninguno de estos artículos, decían que «ya en Santiago no se vendía nada». (Pedro Ruiz Aldea)

un perla

de cuidado te responde «así se habla» cuando lo insultas. pone caras cuando le relatas la muerte de tu madre y escupe el suelo que lustraste. dice haber leído los libros que te hurtaron y anticipa la muerte de tu perro después de una larga enfermedad. se ufana que intercede por ti que no deja de interceder por ti que nunca dejará de interceder por ti para que no te den doble carga laboral. y escribe un oficio donde te acusa de perder el tiempo organizando «campañas del sobre» fraudulentas. te invita un café para aclarar que confundió la z de tu nombre y que acusó al equivocado. jura que enmendará el error que hará justicia que quiere suicidarse. poco después rompe en risa entre tus pares detallando tu cara con su broma «espontánea». te pide tiempo. y no deja de hablar de las distintas concepciones del tiempo.   y de llamarse hernán soruco cardemil.

te citará a reuniones inútiles para inscribirse en tu agenda. para inscribirse en las agendas de tus pocos amigos. para inscribirse en la agenda de todos a los que pueda medrar protagonismo. dirá que el sur es lento. que no conocen a kitano que no leen a yehuda amijai que no hay un persa bío-bío. llamará para pedirte teléfonos, nunca cejará de pedirte teléfonos. postulará ganará te olvidará. conseguirá por tus amigos una patente de alcoholes. un local central. venderá. restaurará comida tailandesa. contratará en negro. saldrá en el diario local regional nacional junto a Perla de Cuidado. dirá que la ciudad es lenta. que las ferreterías se encarecen que la plaza se llena de farmacias que no se apoya a la microempresa. particularmente a la restauración exótica. porque no hay nada que comer porque los aguacates llegan blandos porque venden humitas en la calle. que no aguanta. que feliz un mes en el verano y después de vuelta de donde nunca debió salir. y no se va. aún medra más. tiene muchos empleados. se abrió al rubro de la lencería zapatería y abarrotes. se hizo socia de casas de remates. arma y desarma auspicia. quiere una parcela. quiere un loteo. quiere «algo» frente al río. reclama que no la invitan. que está aburrida. que está escuálido el cóctel.   que quiere elegir autoridad.

otro de aquí

no se para a dejar su plato. habla mal de tu mujer y te pide vino.
quiere un cuchillo «bueno» y te aconseja un sitio donde debes
comprar la carne. ya no le gusta el cordero. ya no le gusta el asado
de tira. vuelve a patear tu macetero. alega contra la maleza el
espinillo los cerdos. te ofrece alambre y un carpintero de ribera. te
explica largamente por qué no sabes de frutales. por qué no debes
de llenarte de avellanos por qué tus hijos se ven flacos. está leyen-
do a los «etnólogos» pero mejor es la novela bélica. llama a las
dos preguntándote por un mecánico. pide que le repitas el nombre
de tu pueblo para comentarlo con su madre. reitera una anécdota
donde te sentiste un desgraciado. llama a las dos para invitarte a
un bingo. recibe a tu mujer de abrazo. le canta le cuenta aprovecha
de preguntarle por su hermana. por el vino.   por su tragedia.

estos de acá [alfredo lefebvre]

delegan todo. dicen: cholito te encargo esto. cuando puedas lo llamas tú. encárgate que me voy a las doce y cuarto. nooooo si es sencillito. es cuestión que te reúnas y le expliques. busca tres cotizaciones. deciden poco ganan mucho viajan demasiado. sus tés son largos. sus reuniones serias. se emborrachan hablando como líderes vecinales municipales del empresariado. detallan lo que hacen. las proyecciones institucionales las críticas que tienen a los pocos aceitados engranajes productivos. aprovechan para pedirte un favorcito. que redactes, que te preocupes, que le avises, que llegaron unas cartas, que quedó algo pendiente.   que «nos representes».

exagera. se engola y opina expone. un caso que dice es emblemáti-
co. su argumento avanza y se interrumpe así mismo con una chan-
za. por lo general inentendible. por lo general ofensiva. cantinflea
driblea dobla. sube el tono logra hacerse entender pide perdón por
la insistencia. colabora con frases como «no es óbice para no feste-
jarlo». «la gallina es la estrategia del huevo para hacer más huevos».
pone comas cuando es cuestión de estilo. su ansiedad lo hace ganar
peso. imita a la cajera hablando con la cajera. no se le ocurre nada
más que comprar frutos secos que ir al médico por su gastritis. por
sus problemas sebáceos por su bruxismo. quiere usar lentes y no
los necesita. pide la palabra y cita erradamente a george simmel a
germán arestizabal. no le prestan atención. cuenta sus problemas
con paradigmas epistemológicos que no ha traducido bien. llama
la atención. logra que le sigan una idea pertinaz y antojadiza que se
rehúsa a desarrollar según confidencia por falta de bibliografía. por
falta de buenas bibliotecas por falta de buenos editores por falta de
buenos investigadores por falta de locales nocturnos. en concier-
tos de cámara tararea golpea la butaca delantera. con su pie con el
programa con su llavero. lo eligen para comités insignificantes.
que cultura que extensión que operación deyse. acepta. le regalan
una entrada al cine.   la extravía.

una liante

de temer. loca de las carteras. de la ubicuidad lupita ferrer. prepara consomés. condumios de necessaire. se sobremaquilla gritando. se sobreafecta planteando. se sobresale informando. reprueba el examen de socialité. pero lame lo que tiene que lamer. busca palco. peor: es una trepa de temer. sus tonos son altos sus tacos son altos. vocea por nada irrumpe por todo. se codea. se cuela. se pone. se ofrece para organizar para segregar para reaparecer para reestructurar para patrocinar.   denle poder.

este de teoría

profesor de birmingham profesor de mehuín huape puringue pobre
profesor de frankfurt reubicado el año 33 en columbia universi-
ty profesor de palo alto trabajando en la isla de la teja pensando si
deja el mental research institute profesor de constanza con aires de
deudor habitacional en parte activo del círculo de viena del grupo
de yale deja consternado a su tesista con aportes obvios del círcu-
lo lingüístico de praga profesor que no contesta sobre los medios
ni las mediaciones que hizo caso omiso a la escuela de tel quel y
el círculo de ardener profesor insuflado por la materia es que pasa
mucha materia es que en un momento comenzó a hablar de los
annales franceses profesor con serias discrepancias con el modelo
de muerte asistida por jubilación profesor que habla de la escena de
avanzada como si hablara de su abuela enferma que fija la vista en
tubos dentífricos en papel lustre en la revista orfeo y la escuela de
santiago haciendo reír con la clásica broma sobre los nombres clavos
sólo para aterrizar a la realidad nacional & regional posicionándose
de la microhistoria italiana mas le espetan le preguntan le critican
le hacen la vida insana gente sobre todo de río negro estudiantes en
su mayoría de la población manuel rodríguez alumnado oriundo de
huelquén que vive en lanco que han venido a estudiar una carrera
que sirva para algo que están pagando la beca en el entendido de
aprender aprendiendo o sea profesor HACIENDO picadillo fino
la reforma y la realidad y que no hay ninguna corriente chilena que
a lo más la escuela quiteña y cuzqueña le nombran a un tal jorge
millas a un h. matucana que nadie le dice que no sabe demás que
sabe pero lo principal le sugieren para el próximo año para el segun-
do evento que en el programa ponga porque no aparecen ciudades
de acá y las palabras «teórico-práctico» y «aplicado a». profesor
entusiasmado. profesor entumecido.   raspado de dios.

palacios navarro

no hay en los pórticos humano más nefasto que el ambulante mete-co. pasa como un extraño y se le reconoce porque carga mercadería «sincera» a menos precio y si de un óbolo se trata todo lo que ofrece lo cambia por un dracma. siempre tiene hambre y aprovecha su acento para dar lástima y conseguir carne salada en el mercado. abusa de la paciencia y son sus exclamaciones mendicantes las que cubren las callejas. el ambulante te dirá: necesita usted un cedé, una cobbata, una peli de terrol. mientras otros de su laya caminan con perrazos mestizos tocando flautas plebeyas. si pasas sin comprar murmurarán a tus espaldas que eres un rácano carajo y si le mandas a azotar se te ofrecerán como esclavos bajo los nylon de almería.

cáeme bien

hará trabajo de campo dirá que lo amarán dirá que construye teoría
desde abajo dirá que sentir es patrimonial que ha descubierto el
teorema del invernadero del turismo rural que a las aves las adormece
con un dedo que los perros aprenden sustentabilidad mediará.
por el transporte atacameño ante el consejo ante el alcalde que lo
importante no es la obsecuencia que lo vital es la sinergia ser una
corchea un poder endógeno uno más de los parientes hidropónicos
al saludar se ve dichoso ganará un puesto en planificación conjugará
todo con local centro local red local historia local capital local
le ofrecerán un curso de posicionamiento geográfico global
lo llamarán lo citarán la agrupación la asociación la comisión
del subcomité de certificación. silbará. reirá.   nos enterrará.

parásitos artificiales

DE: Dirección de Personal
A: Todas las Jefaturas /█████████ y no /█████████ de la Corporación
----

**M O T I V O: Fijar normas para la correcta utilización de Uniformes,
Implementos de Seguridad y de Trabajo/**

El otorgamiento de Uniformes e Implementos de Trabajo, representa un gran esfuerzo humano y financiero para la Universidad, es por ello que es útil establecer algunas políticas que aseguren el uso de estos elementos y se estandarice su utilización. Estos lineamientos se señalan a continuación:

a) Uso Uniforme Escalafones de Secretarias (G) y Administrativos (F)

DIAS	DAMAS	VARONES
Lunes	Uniforme 2002 (blusa color rosado)	Uniforme 2002
Martes	Uniforme 2001 (blusa color celeste)	Uniforme 2001
Miércoles	Uniforme 2002 (blusa estampada)	Uniforme 2002
Jueves	Uniforme 2001 (blusa color damasco o celeste)	Uniforme 2001
Viernes	Uniforme 2002 (blusa color rosado)	Uniforme 2002
•	Actividades oficiales de la Universidad: Uniforme 2002 (blusa estampada) • Se ruega no combinar el Uniforme con prendas que no correspondan a lo que ha sido asignado.	• El Uniforme solo puede ser usado con camisas alternativas, acorde a lo entregado. El resto de las prendas debe mantenerse.

b) Los funcionarios del Esalafón Rondines y Serenos, deberán usar uniforme diariamente.
c. Al resto de los funcionarios se les deberá supervisar el uso correcto de los implementos de trabajo y de seguridad proporcionados por esta Dirección.

Esperamos que estas normativas sean acadadas por nuestros funcionarios y hacemos un llamado a las Jefaturas para que velen por el cumplimiento apropiado de estas disposiciones.

Atentamente,

████████████████

DIRECTOR DE PERSONAL

BD

a los niños se les pega eso

negocio
horizontal

No puede ser mala una mujer que canta*.
Luis Vulliamy

* a Pao

porque

quien ama paga quien llora bala
y sola sana y sabe.

porque quien cava pena quien pasa sea
brea amnio apnea.

porque quien levita lame quien daña cala
sala raspa caldea.

porque quien huye atrapa quien posa afea
pierna piel presea.

porque quien veda evade quien cela rala
cruz cubil cadera.

porque quien soba miente quien escupe mea
mosto mies marea.

porque quien roza queda quien cierra amarra.

no hay

nadie que te lleve esto. un revés de miel y abeja.
una puerta que sella cualquier retorno.
y cuando caiga cuando rebote.
otra hoja triste que se queda blanca
doblada para ti en la incertidumbre.

entonces este pálido dolor que busca señas
esta muesca de olor en la argamasa.

no queda nadie.
en la ciudad sólo espectros con sabor a carne
que no pueden sostener este mensaje.
un telegrama que se apoza
en un extraño perfume de pasillo.

tendrás que extender hacia ti esta mano.
no queda nada
sólo esta bengala húmeda que se dilata
una red de piel parchada.
algo de aceite en las articulaciones de los labios.
manchas de cera para el borde de tu página.

brr

Que cada vez se está más solo de cada lado de la cara . Crujen las patas del enchufe . Hacen *llach* al escupir dos cortes de energía . Y que no quieres ir a ningún recinto que quieres un perro . Pero no te atreves a escuchar ladridos . Que te recuerdan al interruptor de tu habitáculo . *Ruaj-ruaj* rascándote la ceja con una cucharita fría . Abres un párpado y ruegas que no coincida con el otro . Esa visión esa nube rala cuyo hedor te cose los testículos . Los quieres escuchar a todos leyendo poesía . Para seguir burlándote de ti que ya te bañas a menudo con sal . De mar Con sal de ahí con sal fatal . Con sal si tal pero No quieres . Nunca has querido soplar una pelusa del ombligo . Y terminarte el resto de sopa que te queda . Y el otro párpado coincide: es igual: La caja llena de libros y zapatos a Una Caja Llena de Libros y Zapatos . Es un esquirla una pestaña un peso . No te atreves no quieres ir al baño . Sólo quieres jugar un *pac-man* comiendo plastilina . Pero al frente un cuchillo un tenedor una cuchara . *Brag-Brag-Brag-brag* tú eres el mozo tú El invitado la cara del billete con que pagas El que baja las bebidas del camión el que lo conduce Tú el que imprime la guía de despacho. Te quieres ir Te quieres entrevistar para no oírte hablar más estupideces . Pararte en lo que puedes insistir es en pararte Zafarte de esa posición de feto delicado Destullirte Ejercitar el brazo largo tocando algunos timbres Pero no quieres te duelen los zapatos los cordones . No hacen los cordones como antes Como para amarrar el flujo y parar la sangre Es que tú eres el fabricante *il miglior fabbro* Y sólo esperas las doce de la noche para decirle a alguien Tengo Sueño Tengo hambre y está Larkin claro que está Larkin que te dice sólo los jóvenes son libres de estar solos y no te calza porque no eres un Dios Verbal eres un quiste viejo que se embute que se expande en tu lagrimal cansado Y debes salir del amnios pero no alcanzas . Ya no sabes estirar los dedos tienes las uñas rotas tienes la vida rota y el cuello desinflado Y quieres una succión de pena un raspe un gane Te molestan los enchufes de tres patas el color que da la llama en la cocina la distancia entre línea y línea en la baldosa las vueltas del cable del teléfono tu tobillo No miras No buscas en la cama el precipicio Sólo están tus piernas las migas y tus sábanas Te acomodan las migas duras en la espalda el olor que da tu pelo en la frazada . Te tienes arrinconado acurrucado en las aspas de una licuadora Esperando el hielo el agua el azúcar Esperando que llegue alguien y que la encienda Sólo quieres que la encienda Y te bata Y te beba y no frunza el ceño y te orine y hagas algo por ese avellano que se muere . Pero No . El enchufe . Son las patas del enchufe que no entran . No se Prende . Estás ahí entumido al interior de la juguera . *brrr* . frío . solo . El pelo con granos . duros . transparentes . Esperando . entre los cubos Esperando las doce de la noche para decirle a alguien son las doce de la noche.

BK

nnn

*En efecto amigos míos, la cabeza es aquella parte de nuestro ser
con la cual sabemos que estamos tristes (Carlos Droguett)*

(No se teme
al sarro
al barro
ni al hedor de la tetera.

Ni que se pudra
el semen en el bañador.

Y se puede invitar a los amigos
A cerrar

Por fin
Por fuera).

yo

creí acabar con las arañas
que en otro tiempo
acumulaba frente a los frascos de aliño y mermelada
pero siguen circulando y atrapando
pequeños insectos deformes que no buscan
sino morir con luz en la ventana.

he tirado veneno *spray*
para cogerlas cuando se arrastran hacia la cómoda

quiero que cooperes con esta lucha
son más parecidas a ti —le dije

sí. eran cerca de las 13 treinta. no había agua hervida
ni azúcar para revolver adentro de las tazas.
eres una mierda antiambiental —me gritó
todoloquelehacesalentornotelodevolverá
sí. no había refrigerador no había cama
ni la almohada que rellené en otro tiempo
de las cortinas tampoco recuerdo nada.

a mi lado dos o tres cajas con objetos opacos
y las arañas que esperaban por mí en ese vidrio mugriento
en esa cueva vacía.

los clavos estaban apretados en la madera
el viento movía otros poco de viento
la puerta todavía se balanceaba en las bisagras
el agua salía de la llave al resumidero
las moscas hacían un ocho amplio
las ampolletas con asfixia en los soquetes
pero las arañas
las arañas seguían yéndose y viniendo.

en fin esta es mi vida —dijo—

apartando grandes bocanadas de humo con un tic de brazo.

Algo intuía de lo perverso y amargo.

Esta es mi vida y decía de paso

que el umbilical que compartíamos

tenía historia comida terror y espesas confusiones

que nos hacían dos seres

arrastrados por gravedades distintas.

Esta es mi vida —dijo—

diciendo esta frazada este vaso este abismo esta herida que el tiempo retiene y engrosa. Queriendo decir usted no quiera esta inmensa maravilla que sangra. usted se pasa buscando entre su nariz un cuerpo. usted se ha quedado en la tabla del uno. OK. Quería disculparme

pero ella tomó del cuello el globo del que me amarraba.

le dio su habitual empellón salado.

prendió la radio.

lo tocó con una espina.

cuando

al fin pude despertar/ tenía en el borde
de la cama a esa chica que no
saludé en el bar para no meterme en problemas con
mi parche de rencor

lucía shorts/ y el pelo rizado cayendo sobre su cara.
traía un vaso de yogurt y un trozo de durazno sin piel sin imperfecciones en una
vasija con dálmatas pintados
el reloj estaba apagado y por el viento podían ser perfectamente
las 7 de la tarde.

estaba avergonzado/ pegado desde la boca hasta la uretra
por esa faja engomada que niega el beso de la tetilla plana.

el cuarto olía a bestias y se esparcían kilos de ropa muerta.
no puedo creer que estés aquí
no hagas esto por mi derrota —balbuceé
puedo pararme y recolectar maqui y manzanas allá afuera y contarte algunos
viajes de ida y vuelta hacia el averno
(en el borde de la cama ella era un pozo verde una cascada)

— aún puedo freír un huevo.

ella pasó un paño húmedo por mis mejillas y desprendió manchas
que guardaba hace varios meses y que formaban una costra débil
en perpetuo ensanchamiento

estás sano —susurró
quédate a esperar que pase el viento quédate a cicatrizar mis bronquios sólo
quédate a mirar fijo el revés
de esta hoja inmóvil
—contesté

BO

cuando al fin pude despertar/ tenía en el borde de la cama a esa chica del bar
que no saludé/ que cerraba una ventana que se desvanecía
ahora
me anudo solo el corazón de los zapatos.

mmm [waldo rojas]

a stephanie decante & pedro araya

me gusta que los niños lloren. porque se los llevan.

todos

a edwin madrid & aleyda quevedo

quieren que uno vuelva a la normalidad
las cortinas quieren que uno
vuelva a la normalidad
los gordos agotadores quieren que
vuelvas a la normalidad señora
¿quiere que vuelva a la normalidad?
hasta germán el teclado muerto ruega
cuándo pagarás la cuota para la junta de normalidad dígame
sin ambages si le apetece que me dirija
a la oficina central de normalidad a la carpeta
para postular a la normalidad din don bell
el turno de la blanca normalidad
hemmano hemmano regresa por la normalidad
¿me temes? dirá en quito la Mitad del Mundo
dirígete, pues, entonces, antes, a la normalidad
Palabra, en serio ¿quieres que sea rumbo a la normalidad?
es personal pero estarán tranquilos pero estarán a gusto
en fin arguméntenmelo de frente si cesarán
si mañana llego aquí y si mañana me presento estilo
normalidad por ser un dejo quizás un aire
estoy que me convierto hoy mismo
estoy que me hago de una
a la normalidad.

[adrian henri]

Roger McGough
No. Más bien otra monja
Esperando avanzar en
La cola del cine preguntándose
Cómo sería comprar palomitas
Para dos.

de pesar, pesa

de pesar, pesa/ bagatela o roca cursi/ espesa.
de rozar, roza/ ara/ arnea/ retoza
de colar, cuela/ falacia o impostura/ canturrea
de parar, para/ defensa o delantero/ encara

de escribir,

pero déjame terminar

[Durruti]
¡ Demasiados Comités !

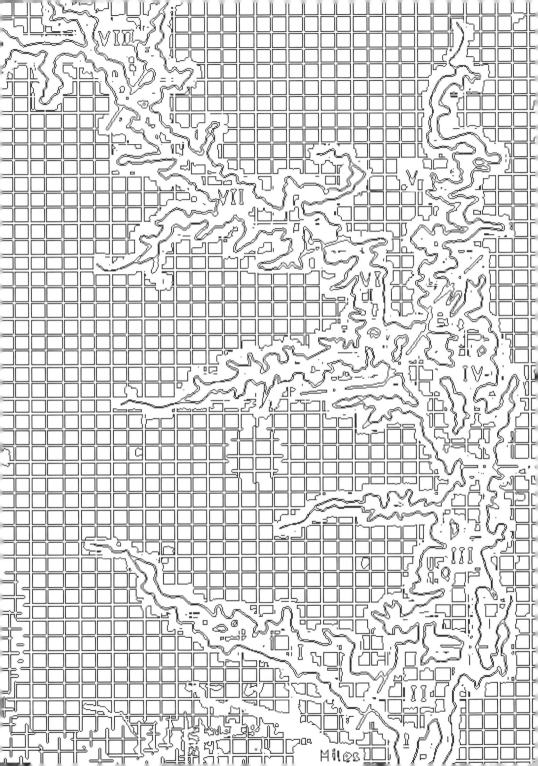

Miles

Translator's Note and Acknowledgments

I first encountered Yanko González's work in 2008 in a bookshop in Santiago, Chile named for his first volume of poetry, Metales Pesados. Yanko, a professor of social and cultural anthropology in addition to being a poet, uses his powers of observation to bring together disparate sources in a resounding patchwork of revelations.

In *Upper Volta*, Yanko uses the former colonial name, Upper Volta (now Burkina Faso), in West Africa to center a dialogue that plays out across street corners, grocery store aisles, and cocktail hours. His use of form, sound, and the language of the everyday, make him one of the most distinctive and important voices writing in Chile today.

As a poet and translator long interested in Southern Cone poetry, I was drawn to Yanko's work because of its ability to reflect the linguistic implications of my own inherent cultural biases. It had a way of extending beyond the specificity of the voices represented in the text, and into a more global language and frame of thought. From my first encounter with this work, I felt driven to bring it to an English speaking audience.

As a result, I've spent the last decade translating *Upper Volta*, striving to preserve not only the uniquely Chilean character of the text, but Yanko's careful use of sound, form, and modes of expression. It has been a pleasure to work directly with Yanko and unravel some of these complexities, where possible, and to leave others for the reader to discover on their own.

Many people helped make the publication of this translation a reality, but none as much as Stacy Doris. Her belief in me, alongside her passion for translation and mentorship are what propelled me to spend the better part of the last decade engaged with *Upper Volta* and with translation in general. Her feedback and constant encouragement inspired me to see the massive importance of Yanko's work, and see it through, year after year. Without her, this translation would not exist in its current form. May her memory live on in these pages.

I would also like to thank Yanko for trusting me with his words. From our very first contact, he has offered nothing but support, enthusiasm, and patient answers to my many questions. I also want to thank him simply for creating such an unapologetic and unique book in *Alto Volta*. His body of work speaks for itself and I feel honored to try and help lend it a voice to reach a wider audience.

Some of the poems in this book have appeared in *A Perfect Vacuum*, *Caesura*, *Changes Review*, the *International Poetry Review*, *Poetry International Archives*, and *Transfer*. I thank the editors of these publications for their support of Yanko's work.

In addition, I'd like to thank Ugly Duckling Presse, in particular, my editors Silvina López Medin and Rebekah Smith for their invaluable feedback, patience, and wherewithal to help finalize the manuscript during the trying times of 2020. Their questions and comments helped unwind some of the more difficult challenges presented by the text, and working together with them was truly a pleasure.

Finally, I want to thank my partner Desiree for her love and encouragement. Thank you for always pushing me to produce the best work possible. Thanks also to my parents, Marc and Judy, for their unwavering, if not unquestioning, support in all my varied pursuits.

Yanko González is a poet and Professor of Social and Cultural Anthropology at the Universidad Austral de Chile. His works include *Metales Pesados*, *Héroes Civiles y Santos Laicos -entrevistas a escritores chilenos-*, *Alto Volta*, *Elabuga*, and *Objetivo General*. González also co-edited the poetry anthologies *Carne fresca: poesía chilena reciente* and *ZurDos: Última poesía latinoamericana*. In 2007, González received the Chilean Critics Award for the best poetry book for *Alto Volta*. His work has been translated into French, English, German, and Dutch.

Stephen Rosenshein is a writer, translator, and visual artist residing in Oakland, CA. He received his MFA in Creative Writing from San Francisco State University. His debut collection of street photography and poetry, *Sincerely, Before*, was published by Clarity Editions and was nominated for the Fine Art Photo Awards in Conceptual Photography. His work has also appeared in the *International Poetry Review*, *Fusion Art*, *Poetry International*, *NAP*, *Chamber Four*, and more. By day, Stephen is a narrative designer and video game writer.